AT JERUSALEM'S GATE
POEMS OF EASTER
By Nikki Grimes

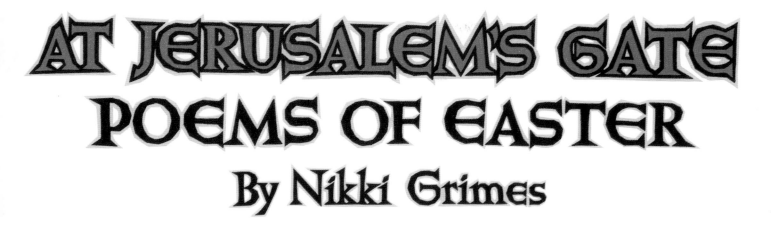

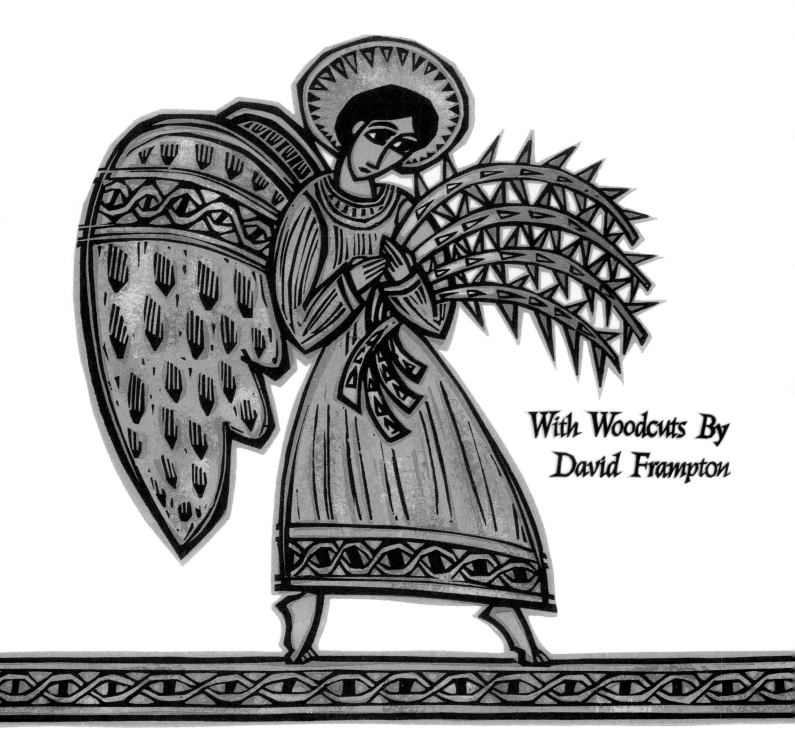

With Woodcuts By
David Frampton

For Ian, Lia, and Gillian Marsh, to remind them of the truth that sets them free

—N. G.

For all the children in all of the world

—D. F.

Text © 2005 by Nikki Grimes
Illustrations © 2005 by David Frampton
Published 2005 by Eerdmans Books for Young Readers
An imprint of Wm. B. Eerdmans Publishing Company
255 Jefferson S.E., Grand Rapids, Michigan 49503
P.O. Box 163, Cambridge CB3 9PU U.K.

05 06 07 08 09   7 6 5 4 3 2 1

Library of Congress Cataloging-in-Publication Data
Grimes, Nikki
At Jerusalem's gate / written by Nikki Grimes ; illustrated by David Frampton.
p. cm.
Summary: A collection of poems which tells the story of the first Easter.

ISBN 0-8028-5183-5 (alk. paper)

1. Easter—Juvenile poetry. 2. Jesus Christ—Passion—Juvenile
poetry. 3. Children's poetry, American. 4. Christian poetry, American.
[1.Easter—Poetry. 2. Jesus Christ—Passion—Poetry. 3.American
poetry.] I Frampton, David, ill. II. Title.
BT482.G75 2003
232.96—dc21
2003001089

The display type was created as a woodcut by David Frampton.
The text type is set in Romano.
The illustrations were created as woodcuts.
Gayle Brown, Art Director
Matthew Van Zomeren, Graphic Designer

Author's Note

For Christians, the resurrection of Jesus Christ is the central theme of Easter—and the cornerstone of the Christian faith.

But there are as many questions in the Easter story as there are answers. Questions like who rolled the stone away? And why didn't Mary Magdalene recognize Jesus? And was Judas predestined to betray Jesus? I don't have the answers, but I think the questions are worth asking, so why not ask them in poetry?

But, first things first. I begin this collection at the gates of the old city where the biblical story of Easter unfolds.

—Nikki Grimes

The story of Easter unfolds when Jesus enters Jerusalem riding on a donkey, as prophesied in Zechariah. Throngs of people there for the Passover Festival met Jesus at the gate, waving palm fronds and singing "Blessed is he who comes in the name of the Lord." They had all heard stories of the miracle worker who had raised Lazarus from the dead, and I imagine religious leaders, like the priest of this poem, were especially eager to catch a glimpse of him.

At Jerusalem's Gate

It's him! shout bands
of rich and poor
who block my view.
I angle for
a glimpse of him
whose touch unlocks
a blind man's sight,
a deaf man's hearing.
There he is! There!
But what is this?
No light shoots from
his fingertips.
His voice calls down
no fire.
And yet, they say
a fig tree withered
at his word.
That he shattered
death's door
not once, but thrice,
calling someone's
loved ones
back to life.
That he speaks
and demons cower.
Perhaps he hides this
power.
He is, by all accounts,
extraordinary, yet
I find him quite ordinary.
Until he turns
and drinks me in.
I gasp, a-tremble,
grasp a palm frond
and wave in a frenzy
of praise and adoration,
singing Hosanna!
Hosanna! Hosanna!
as if my very life
depends upon it.

The religious leaders of Jesus' day enjoyed a degree of influence in Israel. Temple priests received tithes and offerings. The Pharisees and Sadducees were respected men of the community, and few, if any, questioned their spiritual headship—until a man named Jesus came along. He spoke with authority, performed all manner of miracles, and drew crowds wherever he went. What's more, he knew that many priests were corrupt and said so, loudly and often. The priests feared Jesus would soon be receiving the respect—and tithes and offerings—once set aside for them. Consequently, they conspired to rid themselves of the man who threatened their very way of life.

A Conspiracy of Priests

This troublemaker,
rabble-rouser,
thinks he will
disturb the order
by displays of
healing power,
claiming it's of God!

Were he Messiah
we would know it,
though some say
his wonders show it.
We're not fooled
nor yet outdone
by this tradesman's son!

Let us conspire
to quell his fire.
Quick! Before
the crowds that gather
swell in size and
holy fervor
pledging tithes to him.
Judas, turn him in!

Growing up in New York City, I had many Jewish friends. Even among those who weren't particularly religious, Passover was a special holy day. It commemorates the night the angel of death stole all the firstborn sons of Egypt but "passed over" every Jewish house marked with the blood of a lamb. And it was during such a meal in Jerusalem, called the Seder and referred to by Christians as the Last Supper, that Jesus officially assumed the role of sacrificial lamb for all who believed him to be the promised Messiah, the true Lamb of God.

The Passover

It was a borrowed room
in which the thirteen dined.
The fare was bitter herbs,
unleavened bread, red wine,
and lamb to mark the night
Jehovah spared his own
while raining plagues on him
who sat on Egypt's throne.
The holy feast began
accordingly, with prayer,
but then the Lamb of God
poisoned the mood, the air,
with words of blasphemy,
or so they must have seemed:
"I soon will be betrayed
by one of you," said he.
Shaken, eleven men
burst out, "Lord, is it me?"
Meanwhile the traitor crept
unnoticed from the room,
his secret briefly kept.
The question, "Who, Lord, who?"
eclipsed before meal's end.
"I must leave you," said Christ.
"My hour is at hand."
His words made each man choke
for who could swallow then?

Jesus used his final meal with his disciples as a time of instruction. Of all the lessons taught that night, one stands out. During the meal Jesus got up from the table, removed his robe, tied a towel around himself, and with a basin of water went around the table washing the feet of each man present. By doing so, the one they called Son of God gave them a lesson in service no one will forget.

Last Lesson

A gleam in his eye,
the master of surprise
startled the twelve by
rising from the table
and disrobing partway.
He cinched a towel
'round his waist,
then knelt before
each of them in turn.
A basin of water
at the ready,
he bent to wash
their twenty-four
sweaty, gritty feet.
"Mark my example,"
Messiah bid.
"Prove love, as I do.
Serve one another.
Have I not served you?"

Communion focuses on the sacrifice Christ made for all people. The bread is his body, and the wine is his blood. Jesus established this sacrament during the Passover meal. For that reason, communion is also called the Lord's Supper.

Communion

The meal half done,
he tore a loaf
and filled a cup
and blessed them both
then spoke of bread and flesh,
of blood and wine—
four elements by miracle
intertwined.
He'd give himself
for us, he said.
He'd die, then rise,
no longer dead,
and then would come
his kingly reign.
(He made his death
a vow so plain
our hearts refused
to understand.)

This is my body
broken for you.
This is my blood
poured out too.
Do this in
remembrance of me—
Eat. Drink. Live.

Jesus was never more human than when he prayed in the Garden of Gethsemane, wrestling with his own will and God's. It was a familiar spot, one that would be easy for Judas to find, for Jesus and his followers prayed there often. But never had he prayed so intensely, weighing the cost of obeying God and preparing himself for the suffering that lay ahead.

Gethsemane

It was only a matter of time, some say,
before soldiers would come to take him away.
And he prayed and wept, knowing what was amiss,
that his old friend would seal both their deaths with one kiss.
It was only a matter of time.

It was his choice, alone, to fulfill love's command,
to deliver his life into heaven's sure hand.
Should he fight for his freedom, or surrender his will?
God's purpose was perfect, but life was sweet still.
It was always a matter of choice.

It was just a matter of knowing what's best,
to pray for the wicked and weak and to rest
in the quiet assurance that night becomes day,
and soon after soldiers had led him away
he'd die, then arise, having paid for our crimes—
his life now outside of all time.

Names fascinate me. Satan began his existence as Lucifer, or "Light Bearer," heaven's most beautiful angel. Yet, no mother is anxious to name her child Lucifer, for the name has come to represent all that is evil. Which makes me wonder about Judas. What did his name mean? Could the meaning be a key to understanding why he betrayed Jesus? Was it predestination or free will? Questions, questions . . .

What's In a Name?

That night when Christ in agony
knelt praying in Gethsemane
before his march to Calvary
was Judas on his mind?

Was Judas a mere innocent?
A man earmarked for infamy?
Did God choose him for villainy
or did he choose himself?

His name portended prominence:
"Praised Man" his mother baptized him.
But names are what we make of them,
"Betrayer" the badge he earned.

Yet, did Christ in his agony
plead for the soul of one whom he'd
once prayed with in Gethsemane?
Perhaps we'll never know.

After his arrest, Jesus was taken to the home of Caiaphas, where the Sanhedrin, the religious council, convened a tribunal to decide his fate. Nighttime tribunals were illegal, however, and so the council met again the following morning for appearance's sake. The council was determined to have Jesus crucified, and trumped-up charges were the order of the day. Why would false witnesses agree to help provide a legitimate excuse to have an innocent person crucified? My guess is money. Perhaps there were other reasons. Any ideas?

The Gathering

Behind closed doors
we elders, priests, and scribes
gather in the gloom
(liars, all).
Caiaphas surveys the room,
prods a shackled Jesus to the fore
and cries, "Bring on the witnesses!"
In march our well-paid spies.
And what for?
What are we doing here
is a question I swat
like a housefly.
Silent, Jesus stands by
as strangers, poorly rehearsed,
confusing place and time,
recite some dubious crime—

He dines with sinners.
He heals on the Sabbath.
He makes himself equal with God.

"Yes! Yes!" breathes Caiaphas,
a mongrel smelling blood.
"Tell me. Are you the Son of God?"
He licks his lips,
hangs the question like a noose.
Jesus slips it on. "You say that I am."
"Blasphemy! Blasphemy!" we shout.
And yet, doubt nibbles at my ear.
Who is this man, really?
And what are we doing here?

I love a good mystery and the Easter story is full of them. The night before Jesus stood in Pilate's court, Pilate's wife spent hours tossing and turning from a nightmare. She woke with an overwhelming sense of dread and a certainty that the man on trial was innocent. Unable to shake the feeling, she sent a warning to Pilate during the proceedings. What exactly did she dream? I wish I knew!

Pilate's Wife

The dream that robbed my rest
still echoes in my ear
dispatching waves of fear
along my tingling spine.
The dream is drenched in blood,
the details of it gone
like mist by morning's end.
The memory lays me low.
I call my servant, "Quick!
Go to my husband's side.
Confide these warning words:
'Dismiss the one who waits
before your judgment seat.
Spill nothing of his blood
for he is innocent.'"
On this the dream was clear:
there's evil working here.

The Sanhedrin could vote to satisfy the law of Moses, but only Pontius Pilate, Roman Governor of Judea, could order the death sentence, and Rome cared nothing for Mosaic law. Knowing this, the council accused Christ of calling himself King of the Jews, for by Roman law only Caesar could call himself king. Facing the danger of riot and the threat of Caesar's wrath, Pilate gave in to the mob.

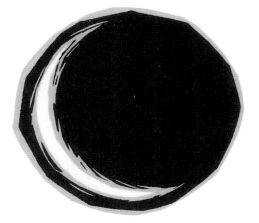

The Net

I ascend the judgment bench,
wrinkle my nose at the vile stench
of political plot born of jealousy,
and declare, "I will set this Jesus free
for I find no cause against him."
The priests, enraged, stir up the crowd,
goad them to protest aloud.
And so, the tug of war begins.
My undernourished conscience
is certain of his innocence,
so I propose a reprimand
but fail to meet the crowd's demand.
"This braggart calls himself a king,
too proud to kiss the emperor's ring.
Is that not a crime in Roman eyes?"
I scan the crowd for Caesar's spies
then ask, "Are you the King of the Jews?
Speak up, man! Why do you refuse?
You do not seem to understand:
Your heart's beat ends at my command."
Scribes and elders lift the cry,
"Free Barabbas! This man crucify!
Kill him who claims to be God's son."
Alarmed, I ask, "Are you the One?"
(My good wife's words come back to me.)
The mob yells, "Do not set him free!"
Frantic, I flog him according to law.
"Look! Here! I have beaten him raw.
Surely your charges are now satisfied."
But the mob shouts, "Let him be crucified!"
Sighing, I wash my hands in their sight.
"His blood be on you this day turned night,
for I find no cause against him."

Face it. Much of the biblical story of Easter makes us squirm, so we rush ahead to the good stuff: the resurrection, the ascension, and the celebration that followed. However, the celebration is hollow unless we pause to consider the price Jesus paid to win the world invitations to the party, and that price included suffering on the way to the cross.

Call It What You Will

Call it what you will—
lash, scourge, whip.
Tipped with its sharp bundle
of spikes and rocks,
it gouged out bits of flesh
until his blood ran
fresh as a river
coursing the length
of his limbs.
Thirty-nine strokes
and then some.
(No one cared to count.)
From the palace of Caiaphas
to the quarters of Pilate,
beating Jesus became
the pastime of the Passion.
Guards and soldiers
eagerly took turns
leaving handprints
on his cheek,
pounding him with rods
while he grew weak,
and, for good measure,
spitting in his face.
Yet, none could erase
that look of pity
or shout down the sound
of his persistent prayer—
"Father, forgive them
for they know not
what they do."

Life is full of coincidences, we say. But are events truly random? I asked myself that question upon discovering that the man named Simon, whom Roman soldiers picked from the crowd to carry Christ's cross, was in fact the father of Rufus and Alexander, two of Christ's own disciples. Here I mention Rufus, whom the book of Romans called "chosen in the Lord."

Simon, Father of Rufus

Is this the one who earned
allegiance from my son?
This youth whose crown of thorns
has sliced his brow like meat?
Sat Rufus at the feet
of this poor broken reed
who stumbles near the gate
too bruised to bear the weight
of his own hanging tree?
He seems serene amidst
this surly, screaming mob,
amidst these wailing wives,
supremely calm for one
walking toward his end.
What's this? Two soldiers rend
me from the jostling crowd
and shift his burden to
my burly shoulders. Am
I here by accident
or divine providence?
(Is it for me to know?)
The man looks up, just so,
and peers into my soul
until he makes me his.
I whisper, "Give me strength,"
measure the path ahead,
the street well-named Sorrow,
and, mourning early, follow.

After Jesus' arrest in Gethsemane, his disciples scattered, fearing their own arrests. Peter hung on the fringes of crowds for news of Christ's fate but denied knowing him personally. As for Christ's other followers, only John and Mary Magdalene, together with Jesus' mother, Mary, dared stand vigil at the cross. Others may have watched from a distance.

From a Distance

The shadow of the thing
was all I saw,
the crosses, three, a blot
against the sky.
I stood far off, awash
in tears and shame,
angry with him—who else
was there to blame?
His promised kingdom seemed
a dream stillborn,
that world in which he'd rule
in peace and light.
For there on Calvary
within my sight
all hope was pierced with him
upon the cross.
What could I do but weep,
for all was lost.

The criminals on either side of Christ were likely highwaymen, robbers who often injured or killed victims in the commission of their crimes. These were rough, foul-mouthed, hard-hearted men. And yet, something about Jesus melted the heart of one of them.

The Highwayman

Even we highwaymen
have heard of him.
The wind carries whispers
of miracle makers to the roadways
we haunt, or used to.
And no matter how
his sentence reads,
I've robbed and roundly beaten
enough innocents to know
he is one.
Besides, the snakes who hiss at him
in this sorry place
are the same who
harried him from the first
(rarely to his face).
I saw them slither after him
many a night, grinning thinly,
jagged stones held tight
behind the neat pleats
of their holy robes.
Damn them! Can't they see
the royalty in his eyes?
I've seen a king or two.
"Remember me when you
come into your kingdom," I say.
He spares a raspy breath,
squeezes out a promise:
"You will be with me
in Paradise this day."
My guilt and fear evaporate.
Content—I never was before!—
I close my eyes to wait
'til we meet at heaven's door.

One of the people caught up in the Passion of Christ was Malchus, servant of Caiaphas, the high priest. When he joined the crowd that went to arrest Jesus in Gethsemane, he never guessed that Peter would slice off his ear, or that the man he came to lead away in shackles would heal him. Did this miracle affect his life? In my imagination, it did. My Malchus never saw Jesus, or himself, the same way again.

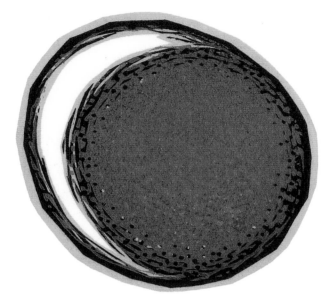

Evidence of Mercy

To hear his master tell it
this Jesus had two heads,
breathed fire at least.
Why else would temple police
and soldiers descend on him
in hordes?
A slave, Malchus could ill afford
to second-guess his master,
and so he joined the others
who swooped upon
the praying band.
"Seize this man,"
signaled Judas with a kiss.
Unwilling to miss their chance,
they rushed forward,
swords glinting in the firelight
of lanterns and torches.
In the madness, a weapon
whistled nearer Malchus
than he knew,
sent his ear sailing.
Jesus, mercy unfailing,
touched his enemy
and then was led away.
Come crucifixion day,
Malchus stood silent
amid the mockers,
rubbing his perfect ear,
ignoring the tear caught
in the corner of his eye,
and puzzled why
one with such power
would consent to die.

Like most mothers, Mary found it difficult to let her child go, and like most children, Jesus didn't feel free to leave this world until he knew his mother would be cared for. This crucial moment took place at the foot of the cross while John, the beloved disciple, stood by.

The Last Goodbye

So, this is how
you have him
wrenched from me—
permitting lying lips,
leather lash,
holy men flinging
fistfuls of anger
sharp as the spikes
that split his sweet muscle,
spoiled his smooth skin.
I'd have gladly laid him
unblemished, unbroken
on the altar, had you asked.
You gave me some sway
in his beginning.
Why not his end?
Look at him.
I could never kiss away
half those bruises.
His countless wounds
would dye
all my cloth crimson.
Besides, these human hands
hold no healing.
Maybe it's best
if I go with John now,
if I say goodbye
and let my son fly
to your arms.

The cross is often referred to as a tree — a poetic reference perhaps, but a tree did provide the material from which the cross was made. According to John's Gospel, Jesus was the Lord of Creation. Among other things, that means the tree on which he hung owed its life to him. I was intrigued by the idea of relationship between Christ and the tree. The first poem led to the second.

Many Questions

What about that tree—
the one that would be
sawn asunder,
its limbs
lashed to a T
to brace his
bruised body?
Did he plant it?
Give it water?
Did he bless
or curse it
like the fig?
As a sapling
did it foresee
a day when nails
would join
its marrow,
its meat,
to the hands
and feet
of the Lord?

One Answer

They made my sturdy limbs
a party to their mutiny.
Forgive Man, Lord,
and me.

Christ was crucified in the middle of the day, yet the sky darkened as if an eclipse were in progress. In the spiritual realm, darkness was temporarily allowed to blot out the light as Christ bore the scars of the sins of the world. God the Father himself could not bear to look at Jesus in that condition. How then could the sun?

Of Course

Of course the sun
refused to gaze
upon the shepherd
wrapped in sin—
a monstrous skin.
How could we see
the heart of him
and know that he
was King?

Jesus was taken down from the cross on Friday evening, the beginning of the Jewish Sabbath, when it is unlawful to do work of any kind, including preparing the dead for burial. He was wrapped in linen and left in a tomb to be properly prepared at a later time. It was Joseph of Arimathea, a wealthy member of the Sanhedrin and secret disciple of Christ, who laid Jesus to rest.

An Act of Kindness

Christ crucified lay limp
as any son undone
by beating, cross, and spear,
a Pharisee the one
to bear him to a place
of rough rock and rest.
Perhaps — this God knows best —
he swabbed away Christ's blood
with tears, the only bath
the Sabbath would allow.
Perhaps he chose instead
to kiss the Master's brow
and whisper his goodbye.
Perhaps he merely wept,
while tired muscles strained
to roll the stone in place
and soldiers sealed it tight
to inch by inch lock out
the air, hope, light.

At dawn on Sunday, with the Sabbath well behind them, several of Jesus' followers went to the tomb to finish preparing his body for burial. Mary Magdalene was among them. When she found his body missing, she was distraught, for while Jesus had spoken of his death and resurrection, who could honestly conceive of it? Certainly not Mary, who met the risen Christ that day and mistook him for the gardener.

Morning Mystery

Dawn alone stood witness
when the weighty stone
was heaved aside.
Then came Mary Magdalene—
crept in,
stumbled out again,
her stare vacant
as the grave,
her loved one missing.
No wonder tears flooded
the banks of her eyes.
"Why do you weep, child?"
a stranger whispered—
the gardener, she thought.
She struggled for air,
wove her worry
into words,
"Sir, tell me
if you know where
they have laid him."
He wrinkled his
thorn-pierced brow
and sighed,
"Dearest Mary."
She knew that voice,
those eyes.
"Master?
Is it you?"

A woman's word didn't count for much in ancient Israel. In fact, the witness of two women counted as only one! Fortunately, Mary Magdalene was not the only person who actually saw the risen Christ. Many of the disciples saw him as well. The Bible records well over 500 witnesses in all. Two of them were men who traveled to the village of Emmaus, seven miles from Jerusalem. Theirs is one journey I would have liked to join!

The Road to Emmaus

They slogged along the road
as if their tears
had turned the dust to mud.
And then he came
skipping questions like
pebbles on a lake.
"Why are you distressed?"
Cleopas explained best.
"Our friend has died,
the one we called Messiah,
mistakenly it seems.
Now women of the faith
feign visions of angels,
or dreams that say
he walks among us—
as if he could!"
The good and patient stranger
pierced their sorrow
with ancient prophecies:

"The dead in Christ will rise.
Messiah will be first
to forge the way."

That evening, when they
were ready and willing to see,
he broke bread,
held it heavenward,
candlelight ringing
the holes in his hands,
and prayed. Like always.

The biblical story of Easter is a record of the miraculous. I imagine there were skeptics surrounding Jesus right up to the ascension itself. One such witness may have been the soldier charged with making certain Jesus died while he hung on the cross.

To Be Continued . . .

Don't tell me he is God.
I pierced his human side,
used my daily-sharpened spear.
In time, I'm certain
someone will explain
how he can be here
preaching still
and rising
on the wings
of the wind.

Notes and References

At Jerusalem's Gate

Mark 11:1-10
John 12:12-15

A Conspiracy of Priests

Matthew 26:1-5,14-16; 28:11-15
Mark 14:55-59; 15:1-5
Luke 22:2-6, 66-71; 23:13-25
John 18:33-19:16

The conspiracy had many players: Judas, disappointed that Jesus was disinterested in overthrowing the Roman Empire, turned him over to the religious council, the Sanhedrin, for thirty pieces of silver.

The Sanhedrin, in turn, convened an illegal tribunal at the palace of Caiaphas, the high priest, to find a legitimate excuse to give Jesus the death penalty.

The following day, Pontius Pilate, Roman Governor of Judea, ordered Christ's crucifixion to appease the Jewish citizens under his authority and thereby avoid a possible rebellion.

In the end, conspiracy extended even beyond the grave. When Jesus' tomb was found empty, the priests bribed the centurion guard to say that Christ's followers had come in the night and stolen his body while they slept.

The Passover

Exodus 12:1-27
Matthew 26:17-29
Mark 14:12-25
Luke 22:1-23
John 13:1-30

Passover is in the first month in the religious Hebrew calendar. This seven-day annual festival was one of three that required all Jews in ancient Israel to travel to Jerusalem for the public celebration.

Last Lesson

John 13:3-15

The Last Supper was an evening of intense instruction for the disciples. The footwashing is noteworthy, however, because it was a lesson by example. Its impact was so powerful that it has reverberated through the ages. The ritual is still practiced in many churches today, usually on Maundy Thursday, during Holy Week.

Communion

Matthew 26:26-29
Mark 14:22-25
Luke 22:14-20

Gethsemane

Matthew 26:36-45
Mark 14:32-42
Luke 22:39-46
John 18:1

The word Gethsemane means "oil press," indicating that it was (most probably) an olive grove itself, or close to a site that was. In any case, it was a peaceful site, suitable for prayer and meditation.

What's In a Name?

Genesis 17:5, 15; 32:28
Mark 14:42-46
Luke 22:3-6
John 13:21-30; 18:2-3

Other people in the Bible whose names changed according to their actions, or as a sign of God's promise, include the following: Jacob to Israel, Abram to Abraham, Sarai to Sarah. Even when no change is indicated, the names of many individuals are significant to the stories written about them.

The Gathering

Matthew 26:57-66
Mark 14:53-64
Luke 22:66-71

Pilate's Wife

Matthew 27:19

The Net

Matthew 27:11-26
Mark 15:1-15
Luke 23:1-25
John 18:28-40; 19:1-16

Pilate was an unwilling actor in the Easter drama. John's gospel records him declaring Jesus' innocence no less than four times. Over and over again Pilate said, in effect, "I find no cause against this man. Is it really necessary to kill him? Are you sure?" The crowd chose to set free Barabbas, an insurrectionist and murderer.

Call It What You Will

Matthew 27:30
Mark 14:65; 15:19
John 19:1-3

Simon, Father of Rufus

Matthew 27:32
Mark 15:2
Luke 23:26
Romans 16:13

Every aspect of crucifixion was cruel, beginning with the fact that those sentenced were forced to carry their own crosses to the crucifixion site. However, Jesus was so badly beaten that he collapsed near the city gate. When soldiers drafted Simon of Cyrene to carry the cross the rest of the way, they didn't realize his sons, Alexander and Rufus, were two of Christ's disciples. Paul called their mother "a mother to me also."

Cyrene, a city in Libya, Africa, was a major Roman outpost.

The street leading to Calvary was Via Dolorosa, literally "the way of sorrows" and is a feature of the "stations of the cross." Pilgrims to Jerusalem walk the stations, fourteen places marking the path Jesus followed to his crucifixion and death. These include Pilate's hall, the garden tomb, and the spot on the Via Dolorosa where Jesus stumbled and Simon took up his cross.

From a Distance

Matthew 26:31
Mark 14:27
Luke 23:49
John 19:23-27, 31-37

While the disciples watched the crucifixion from afar, the Roman centurians stood close by, gambling amongst themselves for Christ's robe. To make certain he died on the cross, they ran a sword through his side, thereby fulfilling the prophecy of Zechariah 13:7.

The Highwayman

Luke 23:39-43

The story of the Good Samaritan found in Luke 10:30-37 helps us understand how robbery might have been considered worthy of the death penalty.

Evidence of Mercy

Matthew 26:51
Mark 14:47
Luke 22:49-51
John 18:10

Peter was a fisherman, not a swordsman. Cutting off the ear of Malchus was most probably the result of a wild swing and a poor aim. Malchus, a slave, not a soldier or policeman, just happened to be standing there.

The Last Goodbye

John 19:25-30

Many Questions, One Answer

Matthew 21:18-20
Luke 13:6-10

Of Course

Matthew 27:45-46
Mark 15:33
Luke 23:44

The most horrific aspect of the crucifixion for Jesus was the total, though temporary, separation from God the Father. While Jesus bore the sins of humankind, his father was unable to look upon him. As God withdrew the light of his presence, it is easy to imagine that the sun itself would likewise willfully withdraw.

An Act of Kindness

Matthew 27:57-60
Mark 15:42-46
Luke 23:50-53
John 19:38

Joseph of Arimathea, at some personal risk, begged Pilate for the body of Jesus. A rich man, Joseph purchased the linen in which Jesus was wrapped and provided the tomb in which he was laid.

Morning Mystery

Mark 16:1-11
John 20:14-18

Mary Magdalene was the first person the risen Christ chose to show himself to. After they had spoken, he instructed her to go and tell the other followers what she had seen and heard. In so doing, she became the world's first missionary.

The Road to Emmaus

Mark 16:12
Luke 24:13-55

To Be Continued . . .

Matthew 28:16-20
Mark 16:19
Luke 24:44-52
John 19:33-34

The site of the ascension was the Mount of Olives, which is also the location of Gethsemane. Christians believe that Christ will one day return, as he promised. This prophesied event is referred to as The Second Coming.